SHIRLITTA BELL

Ultimate Guide to a Career as a Administrative Professional

Exec to Exec - EXECUTIVE ADMINISTRATIVE PROFESSIONALS

This book was professionally typeset on Reedsy.
Find out more at reedsy.com

Contents

1

THE LUCRATIVE CAREER OF THE ADMINISTRATIVE PROFESSIONAL

Explore Your Interests

When deciding if you should attend college or choosing the right career is never an easy task, especially for those who are not sure of what they really want in life, causing many to end up spending, wasting and/or borrowing money for school or choosing the wrong career path that's not what they hoped for or imagined. Some think that their chosen career is what suits them until they realize they don't like or enjoy the career they've chosen. Some people even take the road of a career change which can be a challenging task as well.

Deciding on a career will take reflecting on what you enjoy and researching various career paths. In this book, you will learn about the lucrative career as an Administrative Professional. Whether you are just trying to decide on a career or you have been considering a career change, in this book you will discover the tremendous benefits of pursuing a career in this profession.

An Alternative to College

Benefits offered to administrative professionals by government and corporate agencies often include a comprehensive package aimed at promoting employee well-being, professional development, and long-term financial security. Here are details on some common benefits.

- **Tuition Reimbursement:** Tuition reimbursement programs to support employees' pursuit of higher education and professional development. This benefit typically covers a portion of tuition expenses for approved courses or degree programs related to the employee's job or career advancement.
- **Healthcare Benefits:** Health insurance coverage is a standard benefit provided to administrative professionals. Companies typically offer comprehensive healthcare plans that include medical, dental, and vision coverage for employees and their eligible dependents. These plans may also include options for flexible spending accounts (FSAs) or health savings accounts (HSAs) to help employees manage healthcare expenses.
- **Retirement Plans:** Administrative professionals are often eligible to participate in retirement plans such as the Federal Employees Retirement System (FERS) or the Civil Service Retirement System (CSRS). These defined-benefit plans provide retirement income based on years of service and salary history. Additionally, many government agencies and contracting companies offer employer-sponsored retirement savings plans, such as the Thrift Savings Plan (TSP), which allows employees to contribute a portion of their salary on a tax-deferred basis.
- **Paid Time Off (PTO):** Administrative professionals typically receive paid time off benefits, including vacation days, sick leave, and federal holidays. The amount of PTO may vary based on years of service, employment status (full-time or part-time), and agency or company policies.

- **Flexible Work Arrangements:** Some agencies offer flexible work arrangements, such as telecommuting or flexible hours, to help employees achieve better work-life balance and accommodate personal needs.
- **Training and Professional Development:** Opportunities for training and professional development to enhance the skills and capabilities of administrative professionals. This may include workshops, seminars, online courses, and certifications related to job responsibilities or career advancement.
- **Employee Assistance Programs (EAPs):** EAPs offer confidential counseling, support, and resources to help employees address personal and work-related challenges, including stress, mental health issues, substance abuse, and financial concerns.
- **Employee Recognition Programs:** Companies have employee recognition programs to acknowledge and reward outstanding performance, dedication, and contributions to the organization.

The benefits provided to administrative professionals can indeed offer viable alternatives to pursuing traditional college immediately after high school, whether due to financial constraints or personal preferences. Tuition reimbursement programs enable individuals to enhance their skills and qualifications without the immediate financial burden of college tuition, as they can pursue courses or certifications relevant to their career advancement while working. Health care coverage ensures access to essential medical services and preventative care, easing concerns about healthcare expenses and enabling individuals to focus on their career development. Retirement plans offer long-term financial security and stability, providing a sense of future readiness and reducing the urgency to pursue higher education solely for potential future earnings. Additionally, other benefits such as flexible work arrangements and professional development opportunities contribute to a supportive and conducive work environment where individuals can thrive and grow without the immediate need for college enrollment. These comprehensive benefits packages present attractive alternatives for individuals who may be uncertain about their career paths or prefer gaining practical experience before committing to higher education.

Overall, the benefits package offered to administrative professionals is designed to attract and retain top talent, promote employee satisfaction and well-being, and support professional growth and development. Specific benefits may vary depending on factors such as agency or company policies, employee tenure, and bargaining agreements.

Defining the Role of an Administrative Professional

- **The Unsung Heroes**: Administrative professionals often work behind the scenes, yet their contributions are indispensable to the smooth functioning of any organization.
- **Versatility and Adaptability**: From managing schedules to coordinating meetings, administrative professionals are the backbone of office operations.
- **The Evolving Role**: In today's dynamic workplace, administrative professionals are taking on more strategic responsibilities, becoming key partners in organizational success.

Why Administrative Professionals are Essential in Every Organization

- **Efficiency and Productivity**: Administrative professionals streamline processes, allowing other employees to focus on their core responsibilities.
- **Gatekeepers and Liaisons**: They serve as the first point of contact for clients, vendors, and internal staff, representing the

organization with professionalism and grace.
- **Supporting Leadership**: Administrative professionals enable executives and managers to concentrate on high-level tasks by handling administrative details effectively.

Administrative professionals form the backbone of organizational functionality, operating behind the scenes with indispensable contributions that ensure efficiency and productivity. Their versatility and adaptability are pivotal in managing schedules, coordinating meetings, and serving as gatekeepers and liaisons to uphold the organization's professionalism. In today's dynamic workplace, their role has evolved to encompass strategic responsibilities, making them essential partners in organizational success. By streamlining processes and serving as crucial support for leadership, administrative professionals enable colleagues to focus on core tasks while representing the organization with professionalism and grace in all interactions.

UNDERSTANDING THE ADMINISTRATIVE LANDSCAPE

The Evolution of Administrative Roles

- **Historical Perspective**: Tracing the origins of administrative roles from secretarial positions to the modern-day administrative professional.
  - **Shifts in Responsibilities**: How administrative roles have evolved to encompass a broader range of tasks, including project management, event planning, and strategic support.
  - **Impact of Technological Advances**: The role of technology in reshaping administrative functions and enhancing efficiency in the workplace.

Key Responsibilities and Duties

- **Calendar Management**: Scheduling appointments, coordinating meetings, and managing executives' calendars efficiently.

- **Communication Handling**: Screening calls, responding to emails, and managing correspondence with internal and external stakeholders.
- **Document Management**: Organizing files, maintaining records, and ensuring confidentiality and security of sensitive information.
- **Travel Coordination**: Making travel arrangements, booking accommodations, and preparing itineraries for business trips.
- **Event Planning and Coordination**: Organizing company events, conferences, and seminars, including logistics, catering, and guest arrangements.
- **Office Management**: Overseeing office supplies, equipment maintenance, and facilities management to ensure a conducive work environment.
- **Administrative Support**: Providing administrative assistance to executives, managers, and teams as needed, including preparing reports, presentations, and other documentation.

Different Types of Administrative Positions (e.g., Executive Assistant, Administrative Assistant, Office Manager)

- **Executive Assistants**: Supporting C-suite executives with a wide range of administrative tasks, including strategic planning, decision-making, and communication management.
- **Administrative Assistants**: Providing general administrative support to departments or teams, handling routine tasks, and assisting with day-to-day operations.
- **Management Analysts:** Managing projects from inception to implementation, including coordinating with various stakeholders,

monitoring progress, and ensuring deadlines are met.
- **Office Managers**: Overseeing administrative staff, managing office budgets, and implementing policies and procedures to optimize office operations.
- **Specialized Administrative Roles**: Exploring niche areas such as legal secretaries, medical secretaries, and virtual assistants, each requiring specific skills and expertise.

The evolution of administrative roles spans from historical secretarial positions to today's multifaceted administrative professionals, who handle tasks ranging from calendar management to event planning and strategic support. Technological advances have significantly impacted these roles, enhancing efficiency in the workplace. Key responsibilities encompass calendar management, communication handling, document organization, travel coordination, event planning, office management, and general administrative support. Administrative positions have various job titles, such as Executive Assistants, Administrative Assistants, Program Management Analysts and Office Managers, cater to distinct organizational needs, with specialized roles like legal secretaries and virtual assistants requiring specific skills and expertise.

Breakdown of Salary and Location Data for the Positions of Executive Assistants, Administrative Assistants, Office Managers, and Program Management Analysts
Executive Assistants:

- **Salary Range:** The salary for Executive Assistants can vary based on factors such as experience, location, industry, and the complexity of duties. In the United States, the median annual salary for Executive Assistants typically ranges from $50,000 to $130,000, with variations in high-cost metropolitan areas and industries such as finance and technology.

- Executive Assistant positions are prevalent in major urban centers and business hubs, including cities like New York, San Francisco, Los Angeles, Washington D.C., and Chicago. These locations often offer higher salaries to offset the cost of living.

Administrative Assistants:

- **Salary Range:** The salary for Administrative Assistants varies widely depending on factors such as experience, industry, geographic location, and the scope of responsibilities. In the United States, the median annual salary for Administrative Assistants ranges from $30,000 to $80,000, with higher salaries in industries such as healthcare, finance, and legal services.
- **Location Data:** Administrative Assistant positions can be found in various industries and organizations across urban and suburban areas. Major metropolitan areas and business centers tend to offer higher salaries, but opportunities exist in smaller cities and rural regions as well.

Office Managers:

- **Salary Range:** The salary for Office Managers varies based on factors such as industry, company size, location, and level of responsibility. In the United States, the median annual salary for Office Managers typically ranges from $40,000 to $100,000, with higher salaries in sectors such as healthcare, finance, and technology.
- **Location Data:** Office Manager positions are available in diverse industries and organizations across urban and suburban regions.

Major metropolitan areas and commercial centers often offer higher salaries, but opportunities exist in smaller cities and towns as well.

Program Management Analysts:

- **Salary Range:** The salary for Program Management Analysts depends on factors such as experience, education, industry, location, and the complexity of projects managed. In the United States, the median annual salary for Program Management Analysts typically ranges from $60,000 to $130,000, with variations based on industry sectors such as government, healthcare, IT, and consulting.
- **Location Data:** Program Management Analyst positions are prevalent in government agencies, consulting firms, healthcare organizations, and IT companies, with concentrations in major metropolitan areas, technology hubs, and government centers such as Washington D.C., New York, San Francisco, and Boston. These locations often offer higher salaries to offset the cost of living and demand for specialized skills.

3

SKILLS AND QUALITIES OF SUCCESSFUL ADMINISTRATIVE PROFESSIONALS

Communication Skills: Written and Verbal

Written Communication:

- Crafting clear, concise, and professional emails, memos, and reports.
- Ensuring proper grammar, punctuation, and formatting in written communication.
- Conveying information effectively to diverse audiences.

Verbal Communication:

- Articulating ideas and instructions clearly and confidently.
- Active listening to understand and address colleagues' concerns and queries.
- Handling phone calls and in-person interactions with professional-

ism and tact.

Organization and Time Management:

- Prioritizing tasks based on deadlines and importance.
- Maintaining orderly and efficient filing systems for documents and records.
- Creating schedules and calendars to manage meetings, appointments, and deadlines effectively.
- Anticipating potential conflicts or bottlenecks and proactively addressing them to ensure smooth operations.

Attention to Detail and Problem-Solving Abilities:

- Paying close attention to accuracy and precision in tasks and documentation.
- Identifying errors or discrepancies and taking prompt corrective action.
- Analyzing problems systematically and devising practical solutions.
- Being resourceful and creative in resolving challenges that arise in daily operations.

Technological Proficiency:

- Proficiency in using standard office software such as Microsoft Office Suite (Word, Excel, PowerPoint, Outlook) and Google Workspace.
- Familiarity with specialized software and tools relevant to administrative tasks, such as project management software or CRM systems.
- Basic troubleshooting skills to address common technical issues

independently.

- Willingness to learn and adapt to new technologies and software updates.
- Timekeeping Software such as Deltek Costpoint
- Travel Software such as Defense Travel System (DTS) and E2 Travel
- On-boarding / Out-processing Systems
- Training Software

Adaptability and Flexibility:

- Remaining composed and adaptable in fast-paced and dynamic work environments.
- Willingness to take on new responsibilities and learn new skills as required.
- Handling unexpected changes or disruptions with resilience and professionalism.
- Collaborating effectively with colleagues from diverse backgrounds and adapting communication styles as needed.

Successful administrative professionals demonstrate a combination of these skills and qualities, enabling them to navigate challenges, communicate effectively, and contribute to the efficiency and success of their organizations. Continuously honing and refining these skills can lead to increased effectiveness and opportunities for advancement in the administrative profession.

4

CAREER PATHS AND OPPORTUNITIES

Advancement Opportunities within the Administrative Field

- Administrative Assistant to Executive Assistant: Progression from supporting a team to supporting high-level executives, often involving more complex tasks and increased responsibilities.
  - Office Coordinator to Office Manager: Transitioning from overseeing day-to-day operations to managing administrative staff, budgets, and office procedures.
  - Administrative Specialist to Administrative Supervisor: Assuming leadership roles with responsibility for training, supervising, and evaluating administrative staff members.
  - Program Management Analyst: Responsible for identifying problems within an organization and proposing solutions to improve efficiency, reduce costs, and increase profits. They analyze financial and operational data, conduct interviews with employees and managers, and observe organizational processes to understand current procedures and identify areas for improvement. Manage-

ment analysts also develop recommendations and present findings to management for implementation.

Transitioning to Specialized Roles (e.g., Legal Secretary, Medical Secretary, Security Cleared Administrative Professionals)

- Legal Secretary: Providing administrative support within law firms or legal departments, including drafting legal documents, maintaining case files, and scheduling court appearances.
- Medical Secretary: Assisting healthcare professionals with administrative tasks such as scheduling appointments, managing patient records, and processing insurance claims.
- Executive Secretary: Supporting top-level executives in various industries with tasks such as managing calendars, arranging travel, and coordinating meetings and events.
- Security Cleared Administrative Professionals: Security cleared administrative professionals play a critical role in various sectors, especially those requiring adherence to strict confidentiality and security protocols. They perform tasks such as managing calendars, scheduling meetings, handling correspondence, and organizing documents, all while ensuring compliance with security clearance requirements. These professionals may work in government agencies, defense contractors, intelligence organizations, or other sectors where security clearance is essential.

Entrepreneurial Ventures for Administrative Professionals

- Virtual Assistant: Offering administrative services remotely to clients, including email management, scheduling, bookkeeping, and social media management.
- Freelance Administrative Consultant: Providing expertise in ad-

ministrative processes, systems, and organization to businesses on a contract basis.

- Administrative Training and Coaching: Sharing knowledge and skills with aspiring administrative professionals through workshops, webinars, and coaching programs.

Transitioning to specialized roles allows administrative professionals to leverage their skills and experience in specific industries or areas of expertise. Additionally, entrepreneurial ventures provide opportunities for autonomy, flexibility, and potentially higher earnings. With the right qualifications, networking, and entrepreneurial spirit, administrative professionals can explore diverse career paths and carve out fulfilling professional journeys tailored to their interests and goals.

5

NAVIGATING CHALLENGES IN THE WORKPLACE

Dealing with Office Politics

- Recognize the Dynamics: Understand the informal power structures, alliances, and communication channels within the organization.
- Maintain Neutrality: Avoid taking sides or engaging in gossip that could compromise professional relationships.
- Focus on Work: Keep the focus on tasks and objectives rather than personal agendas or office politics.
- Build Relationships: Cultivate positive relationships with colleagues based on mutual respect and professionalism.

Managing Stress and Burnout

- Identify Stress Triggers: Recognize signs of stress and identify specific triggers such as workload, deadlines, or interpersonal conflicts.

- Practice Self-Care: Prioritize activities that promote physical and mental well-being, such as exercise, mindfulness, and hobbies.
- Set Boundaries: Establish clear boundaries between work and personal life to prevent burnout and maintain a healthy balance.
- Seek Support: Reach out to supervisors, colleagues, or professional counselors for support and guidance during challenging times.

Handling Difficult Situations and Conflict Resolution

- Stay Calm and Objective: Maintain composure and approach conflicts with a calm and rational mindset.
- Active Listening: Listen actively to understand the concerns and perspectives of all parties involved in the conflict.
- Find Common Ground: Identify areas of agreement and explore potential solutions that address the interests of everyone involved.
- Communicate Effectively: Express concerns and feedback clearly and constructively, focusing on behaviors and actions rather than personal attacks.

Dealing with office politics requires diplomacy, discretion, and a focus on maintaining professionalism and integrity. Managing stress and burnout involves self-awareness, self-care practices, and seeking support when needed. Handling difficult situations and conflict resolution entails effective communication, active listening, and a collaborative approach to problem-solving. By developing these skills and strategies, administrative professionals can navigate workplace challenges with confidence and resilience, contributing to a positive and productive work environment.

6

PROFESSIONAL DEVELOPMENT AND CONTINUOUS LEARNING

Pursuing Certifications and Training Programs

- Identify relevant certifications such as Certified Administrative Professional (CAP) or Microsoft Office certifications.
- Explore training programs in areas like project management, communication skills, or software proficiency.
- Leverage online platforms like LinkedIn Learning, Coursera, or Udemy for flexible learning options.

Networking and Building Professional Relationships

- Attend industry events, conferences, and networking mixers to connect with peers and mentors.
- Join professional organizations such as the International Association of Administrative Professionals (IAAP) for networking opportunities and resources.
- Engage in online communities and forums to share insights, ask

questions, and learn from others in the field.

Staying Updated with Industry Trends and Technologies

- Follow industry blogs, newsletters, and publications to stay informed about emerging trends and best practices.
- Participate in webinars, workshops, and seminars focused on technological advancements and industry innovations.
- Experiment with new software tools and productivity apps to streamline workflows and stay competitive.

Balancing Work and Personal Life

- Setting Boundaries: Establish clear boundaries between work and personal time to prevent burnout and maintain well-being.
- Time Management Techniques: Prioritize tasks, set realistic goals, and use time-blocking or using Pomodoro Techniques (a time management plan) to enhance productivity.
- Self-Care and Wellness Strategies: Incorporate regular exercise, mindfulness practices, and hobbies into your routine to recharge and reduce stress.
- Success Stories and Insights from Experienced Administrative Professionals: Learn from the experiences and journeys of seasoned professionals through interviews, profiles, and case studies.

Interviews and Profiles of Successful Administrators

- Gain insights into the career paths, challenges, and triumphs of successful administrative professionals.
- Learn valuable lessons and glean practical advice for navigating the administrative profession.

- Draw inspiration from success stories and diverse career trajectories within the field.

Resources and Tools for Administrative Professionals

- Recommended Books, Websites, and Online Communities: Discover curated resources and online communities tailored to administrative professionals' needs.
- Software and Apps for Productivity and Organization: Explore tools such as Microsoft OneNote, Trello, Asana, or Evernote for task management, and Slack or Microsoft Teams for team collaboration.

Continual learning and professional development are essential for staying relevant and thriving in the administrative profession. By investing in certifications, networking, and staying updated with industry trends, administrative professionals can enhance their skills, expand their opportunities, and achieve long-term success in their careers.

7

BALANCING WORK AND PERSONAL LIFE

Setting Boundaries

- Define Clear Work Hours: Establish specific start and end times for work to delineate between professional and personal time.
  - Communicate Expectations: Clearly communicate availability and response times to colleagues and supervisors to manage work-related expectations.
  - Limit After-Hours Work: Resist the urge to constantly check emails or respond to work requests outside of designated work hours to maintain a healthy work-life balance.
  - Learn to Say No: Prioritize tasks and commitments, and politely decline additional responsibilities or requests when necessary to avoid overcommitting.

Time Management Techniques

- Prioritize Tasks: Identify high-priority tasks and tackle them first to ensure critical work is completed efficiently.

- Organize Your Work Email Inbox:Create folders under your Inbox for specified topics, such as Calendar, Correspondence, Travel, Information Technology, Training, Awards, etc. and file the emails accordingly in perspective folders and leave the follow-up emails that require attention and closure in your Inbox until complete – then move to the perspective folder.
- Use Time Blocking: Allocate specific blocks of time for different tasks or activities to minimize distractions and increase productivity.
- Set Realistic Goals: Break down larger tasks into smaller, manageable goals to maintain focus and momentum throughout the day.
- Leverage Technology: Utilize productivity tools and apps such as calendars, task managers, and project management software to organize tasks and deadlines effectively.

Self-Care and Wellness Strategies

- Schedule Breaks: Take regular breaks throughout the workday to recharge and avoid burnout, whether it's a short walk, stretching, or meditation.
- Maintain Healthy Habits: Prioritize nutritious meals, adequate hydration, and regular exercise to support physical and mental well-being.
- Practice Stress Management: Incorporate stress-relief techniques such as deep breathing exercises, mindfulness, or journaling to manage stress levels effectively.
- Invest in Hobbies and Interests: Allocate time for activities outside of work that bring joy and fulfillment, whether it's hobbies, spending time with loved ones, or pursuing personal interests.

Balancing work and personal life requires an intentional effort and proactive strategies to protect personal time, manage workload effectively, and prioritize self-care. By setting boundaries, practicing time management techniques, and prioritizing self-care, individuals can achieve a harmonious balance between their professional and personal responsibilities, leading to improved well-being and overall satisfaction in both aspects of life.

8

SUCCESS STORIES AND INSIGHTS FROM EXPERIENCED ADMINISTRATIVE PROFESSIONALS

Interviews and Profiles of Successful Administrators

- Gain valuable insights into the career journeys, challenges faced, and accomplishments achieved by seasoned administrative professionals through in-depth interviews and profiles.
- Learn about the diverse backgrounds, career paths, and strategies employed by successful administrators to excel in their roles.
- Explore the experiences and perspectives of administrators across various industries and organizational settings to gain a holistic understanding of the profession.

Lessons Learned and Career Advice

- Discover practical lessons learned from experienced administrative professionals as they reflect on their career experiences and

milestones.
- Benefit from valuable career advice, tips, and strategies shared by successful administrators for navigating challenges and seizing opportunities in the administrative profession.
- Gain insight into effective communication techniques, time management strategies, and professional development pathways that have contributed to the success of experienced administrators.

By delving into success stories and insights from experienced administrative professionals, aspiring and current administrators can glean valuable wisdom, inspiration, and actionable advice to propel their own careers forward. These interviews and lessons learned offer a wealth of knowledge and guidance for navigating the complexities of the administrative profession and achieving long-term success and fulfillment in the field.

9

RESOURCES AND TOOLS FOR ADMINISTRATIVE PROFESSIONALS

Recommended Books, Websites, and Online Communities

- Explore a curated list of books that cover topics ranging from time management and communication skills to leadership and professional development specifically tailored to administrative professionals.
  - Access reputable websites and online platforms offering articles, guides, and resources relevant to the administrative profession, including tips for improving efficiency, managing workload, and advancing careers.
  - Engage with online communities and forums dedicated to administrative professionals, where members can ask questions, share insights, and connect with peers facing similar challenges and opportunities.

Software and Apps for Productivity and Organization

- Discover a variety of software tools and applications designed to enhance productivity, streamline workflows, and improve organization for administrative professionals.

- Utilize project management software such as Trello, Asana, or Monday.com to manage tasks, deadlines, and collaborative projects effectively.
- Explore tools like Evernote, Microsoft OneNote, or Notion for note-taking, document organization, and information management, enabling seamless access to important data and resources.
- Leverage communication and collaboration platforms such as Microsoft Teams, or Zoom for efficient team communication, file sharing, and virtual meetings in both remote and office settings.

Access to recommended books, websites, online communities, and software tools empowers administrative professionals to stay informed, connected, and productive in their roles. By leveraging these resources and tools, administrators can enhance their skills, streamline workflows, and contribute to the success of their organizations effectively.

10

RECOMMENDED BOOKS, WEBSITES, AND ONLINE COMMUNITIES

- **Books:** Access a comprehensive list of recommended books covering a wide array of topics relevant to administrative professionals, including time management, communication skills, and leadership development. Books like "Eat That Frog!" by Brian Tracy and "The 7 Habits of Highly Effective People" by Stephen Covey offer invaluable insights and strategies for personal and professional growth.
- **Websites:** Explore reputable websites catering to administrative professionals, such as Administrative Professional Today and Office Dynamics, which provide articles, tips, and resources to support skill development and career advancement. These platforms often feature articles on industry trends, best practices, and success stories from experienced professionals.
- **Online Communities:** Join online communities and forums specifically tailored to administrative professionals, such as LinkedIn groups or Reddit communities. These platforms offer opportunities to engage with peers, share experiences,

ask questions, and seek advice from a supportive network of professionals facing similar challenges and opportunities.

Software and Apps for Productivity and Organization

- **Project Management Tools:** Utilize project management software like Asana, Trello, or Basecamp to organize tasks, track deadlines, and collaborate with team members efficiently. These tools allow administrative professionals to create task lists, assign responsibilities, and monitor project progress in real-time.
- **Note-Taking Apps:** Streamline note-taking and information organization with apps like Evernote, Microsoft OneNote, or Google Keep. These tools enable users to capture ideas, create to-do lists, and store important documents across various devices, ensuring easy access and retrieval of information.
- **Communication Platforms:** Enhance team communication and collaboration with platforms such as Microsoft Teams or Zoom. These tools facilitate instant messaging, video conferencing, and file sharing, enabling seamless communication and coordination among team members, whether in-office or remote.

By leveraging recommended books, websites, online communities, and software tools, administrative professionals can access valuable resources and enhance their skills, productivity, and effectiveness in the workplace. These resources empower professionals to stay informed, connected, and organized, ultimately contributing to their success and growth in the administrative field.

11

CONCLUSION

Always in Demand

The demand for administrative professionals remains consistently high across various industries and sectors due to their integral role in supporting organizational operations. Here are some key factors contributing to the ongoing demand for administrative professionals:

- **Essential Functions:** Administrative professionals perform essential functions such as managing schedules, coordinating meetings, handling communications, and maintaining records. These tasks are critical for the smooth functioning of organizations, regardless of their size or industry.
- **Business Growth:** As businesses grow and expand, the need for administrative support often increases. Additional staff, departments, and projects require efficient coordination and management, driving the demand for skilled administrative professionals.
- **Specialized Expertise:** With advancements in technology and changes in work practices, there is a growing demand for ad-

ministrative professionals with specialized skills. For example, proficiency in office software, project management tools, and communication platforms is highly sought after in today's digital workplace.

- **Focus on Efficiency:** Organizations are constantly seeking ways to improve efficiency and productivity. Administrative professionals play a key role in streamlining processes, optimizing workflows, and reducing administrative overhead, contributing to overall organizational effectiveness.

- **Regulatory Compliance:** Many industries, particularly those in highly regulated sectors such as healthcare, finance, and government, have strict compliance requirements. Administrative professionals help ensure that documentation, reporting, and administrative practices adhere to regulatory standards, mitigating risks and ensuring legal compliance.

- **Support for Executives:** Senior executives and managers rely heavily on administrative support to manage their busy schedules, coordinate activities, and handle administrative tasks. As organizations recognize the importance of executive productivity, the demand for skilled executive assistants and administrative professionals continues to grow.

- **Remote Work Trends:** The shift towards remote and hybrid work models, accelerated by technological advancements and the COVID-19 pandemic, has increased the demand for administrative professionals who are adaptable to virtual work environments. Remote administrative support is essential for maintaining organizational efficiency and collaboration across dispersed teams.

Embracing the Role of an Administrative Professional

- Recognize the importance and value of the administrative profession in supporting organizational efficiency, productivity, and success.

- Embrace the diverse responsibilities and challenges inherent in the role of an administrative professional, from managing calendars and correspondence to facilitating communication and coordination within the workplace.
- Cultivate a sense of pride and purpose in contributing to the smooth operation and overall effectiveness of the organizations and teams you support.

The Future of Administrative Careers

- Acknowledge the evolving nature of administrative roles in response to technological advancements, changing workplace dynamics, and shifting organizational needs.
- Anticipate emerging trends such as remote work, virtual collaboration tools, and automation shaping the future landscape of administrative careers.
- Embrace opportunities for professional growth, skill development, and adaptation to remain relevant and competitive in the evolving administrative landscape.

Overall, the demand for administrative professionals is expected to remain strong as businesses continue to evolve, adapt to changing work environments, and prioritize efficiency and productivity. Professionals who possess a combination of administrative skills, technological proficiency, and adaptability to changing work trends are well-positioned to meet the ongoing demand in this dynamic field.

Popular Job Search Websites

- **Indeed**

Features: Indeed aggregates job listings from thousands of websites, including company career pages, job boards, and recruitment agencies. Users can search for jobs by keyword, location, salary, and company, and filter results by job type, experience level, and more. Indeed also offers resume posting, company reviews, salary information, and career advice resources.

Benefits: Extensive job listings across various industries and locations, user-friendly interface, customizable job alerts, and access to employer reviews and salary insights.

- **LinkedIn**

Features: LinkedIn is a professional networking platform that also serves as a job search website. Users can create profiles highlighting their skills, experience, and education, connect with professionals and recruiters, and search for job opportunities posted by companies. LinkedIn offers job recommendations based on user profiles, as well as features for networking, professional development, and industry insights.

Benefits: Access to a vast network of professionals and recruiters, personalized job recommendations, visibility to employers, and opportunities for networking and career growth.

- **Glassdoor**

Features: Glassdoor provides job listings, company reviews, salary reports, and interview insights contributed by current and former employees. Users can search for jobs by keyword, location, company, or job title, and access detailed company profiles, including ratings and reviews on company culture, leadership, and compensation.

Benefits Transparent insights into company culture and salaries, access to job listings and interview reviews, personalized job alerts, and career advice resources.

- **Monster:**

Features: Monster is a popular job search website offering a wide range of job listings across various industries and locations. Users can search for jobs by keyword, location, industry, and job type, and upload resumes for employers to view. Monster also provides career advice articles, resume writing services, and tools for job seekers.

Benefits: Extensive job listings, resume posting services, career resources, and job search tools such as personalized job alerts and application tracking.

- **ZipRecruiter:**

Features: ZipRecruiter aggregates job listings from multiple sources and uses AI-powered algorithms to match candidates with relevant job opportunities. Users can create profiles, upload resumes, and apply to jobs directly through the platform. ZipRecruiter offers job alerts, resume search for employers, and mobile apps for job seekers.

Benefits: Simplified job search process, personalized job recommendations, mobile-friendly interface, and access to a wide range of job listings.

- **Virtual Vocations:**

Features: Virtual Vocations specializes in remote and telecommute job opportunities across various industries and job categories. Users can search for remote jobs by keyword, location, job type, and industry, and access resources for remote job seekers, including tips for finding and succeeding in remote work.

Benefits: Focus on remote job opportunities, curated listings for telecommute positions, access to remote job search resources and guides.

These job search websites offer valuable resources and tools for job seekers, including comprehensive job listings, networking opportunities, career advice, and insights into company culture and salaries. Depending on individual preferences and career goals, job seekers can leverage these platforms to find suitable job opportunities and advance their careers.